Breakfast on the

Cock-a-doodle-doo!
Wake up! Wake up!
It is breakfast time.

The hens are hungry.
The farmer feeds the hens.

4

The cows are hungry.
The farmer feeds the cows.

The sheep are hungry.
The farmer feeds the sheep.

The pigs are hungry.
The farmer feeds the pigs.

The horses are hungry.
The farmer feeds the horses.

The farmer feeds the cats.
The farmer feeds the dogs.

The farmers are hungry, too.
It is breakfast time!